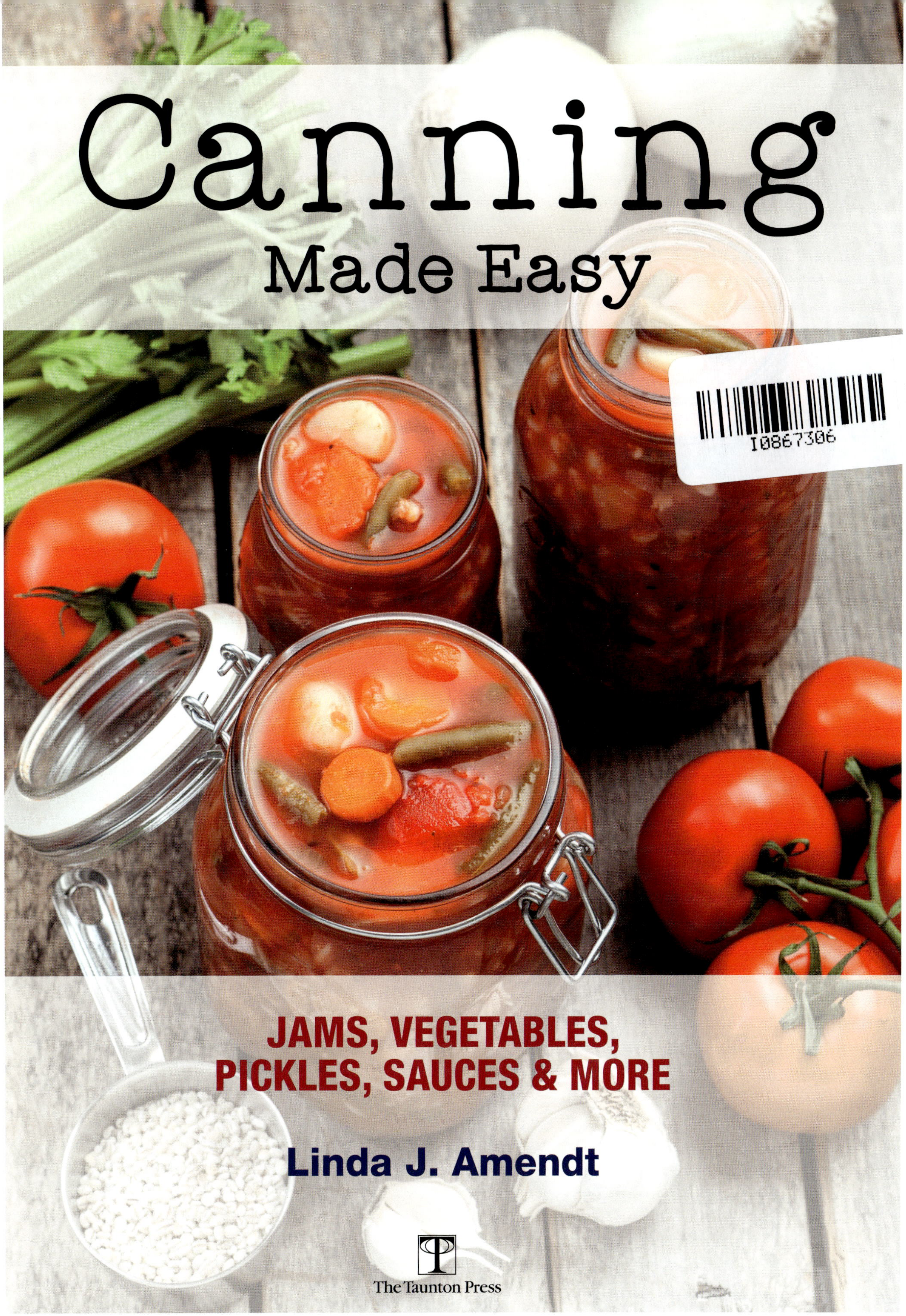

# Canning
## Made Easy

**JAMS, VEGETABLES, PICKLES, SAUCES & MORE**

**Linda J. Amendt**



The Taunton Press

PRODUCED EXCLUSIVELY FOR LEISURE ARTS, INC., MAUMELLE, ARKANSAS

Content excerpted from *Blue Ribbon Canning* by The Taunton Press
(ISBN-13 978-1-62710-769-3; copyright 2015). Used by permission.


The Taunton Press, Inc., 63 South Main Street, PO Box 5506, Newtown, CT 06470-5506
email: tp@taunton.com

Editor: Carolyn Mandarano
Copy Editor: Li Agen
Indexer: Heidi Blough
Interior design and layout: Rita Sowins / Sowins Design
Photographer: Andrew Purcell, except pp. 1, 8, 28, 34, 36, 44, 47, and book covers.
Food Stylist: Carrie Purcell
Prop Stylist: Paige Hicks



EDITORIAL STAFF
Senior Product Director: Pam Stebbins
Creative Art Director: Katherine Laughlin
Publications Director: Leah Lampirez
Special Projects Director: Susan Frantz Wiles
Art Category Manager: Lora Puls
Graphic Artist: Cailen Cochran
Prepress Technician: Stephanie Johnson
Contributing Photographer: Ken West
Contributing Photo Stylist: Sondra Daniel

BUSINESS STAFF
President and Chief Executive Officer: Fred F. Pruss
Senior Vice President of Operations: Jim Dittrich
Vice President of Retail Sales: Martha Adams
Chief Financial Officer: Tiffany P. Childers
Controller: Teresa Eby
Information Technology Director: Brian Roden
Director of E-Commerce: Mark Hawkins
Manager of E-Commerce: Robert Young

Special Edition ISBN-13/EAN 978-1-4647-4289-7 © 2015 by Leisure Arts, Inc., 104 Champs Blvd., STE 100, Maumelle, AR 72113-6738, www.leisurearts.com. 

# * Introduction *

Home canning is seeing a huge resurgence. What was once a necessity to preserve food for the long, hard winter, canning has become a popular hobby and even a year-round way of life for new generations. No longer the domain of grandmothers with large gardens, canners now come in all ages and from all backgrounds. You will find a wealth of canners in every state and every community, ranging in age from young children to seniors. Many people find canning a relaxing and enjoyable activity. We also like the satisfaction of preparing the canned goods ourselves and knowing what is in the food we feed to our families. Let's get canning!

# CONTENTS


Ingredients .... 4
Canning Equipment .... 8
Canning Techniques .... 12
Processing Canning Jars .... 20
Jams, Jellies, Syrups & Marmalades . 28
- Simple Fruit Jam .... 31
- Pear Lime Jam .... 32
- Wine Jelly .... 33
- Berry Syrup .... 34
- Red Onion Marmalade .... 35

Pickles, Relishes, Sauces & Salsas .... 36
- Barb's Bread-and-Butter Pickles .... 39
- Corn Relish .... 40
- Sweet and Tangy Tomato Relish .... 41
- Tomato Basil Sauce .... 42
- Roasted Corn and Sweet Pepper Salsa .... 43

Fruits & Vegetables .... 44
- Peach Halves .... 47
- Vegetable Soup .... 48

Metric Equivalents .... 49

# * Ingredients *

The quality of the ingredients you use for putting up jams, pickles, sauces, vegetables, and all things canned has a direct effect on the outcome of the finished product. Ingredients play an important role in determining the intense flavor, appropriate texture, and vibrant color that are characteristic of great canned foods. Everything from the fruits and vegetables to the sugar, vinegar or lemon juice, herbs, and any other ingredients and flavorings will all have an impact on your results. When canning, always use the best and freshest ingredients available. Don't skimp on quality or you may be disappointed with the results.

## Produce

Fruits and vegetables are the primary ingredients in canning recipes. They provide the main source of flavor and help determine the texture of the finished product. The flavor and texture of your canned items will only be as good as the flavor and texture of the fruits and vegetables you put into them, so start with produce that is in season and at its peak of ripeness. Avoid using fruits or vegetables that are underripe, which have a mild flavor and very firm texture, or are overripe, which can have an "off" flavor and soft texture. Whenever possible, choose produce as soon as possible after harvest—while some fruits and vegetables last longer than others, all are at their peak within 12 to 24 hours after being picked.

Be sure the fruits and vegetables you choose are free of bruises and blemishes. Bruised or damaged fruit may contain harmful bacteria that could contaminate your canned item. Soft fruit can also affect the texture of a jam or marmalade and may prevent the spread from setting.

## Sugar

Sugar serves many purposes in canning and is an essential ingredient in preserving fruit, no matter what type of canned item you're making. Sugar obviously adds sweetness, but it also acts as a preservative in canned fruits, pickles, and soft spreads by inhibiting the growth of microorganisms in the jars during storage. Sugar also enhances the flavor of fruit, helps fruit maintain both its shape and texture, and aids in the gel formation that allows a spread to set. Don't reduce the amount of sugar called for in a soft spread recipe—not only will it prevent the spread from setting, but it can also allow yeasts and molds to grow in sealed jars.

## Pectin

Pectin is a water-soluble carbohydrate and natural thickening and gelling agent found in the tissues of all fruits. Some fruits, such as apples, grapes, gooseberries, and cranberries, have a naturally high level of pectin, while others, such as strawberries, cherries, pears, and pineapple, have a low pectin content. Pectin develops as fruit ripens, and the highest levels of pectin are found in fruit that is slightly underripe. The pectin found in fruit that is significantly underripe or fruit that is overripe will not form a strong gel. Commercial pectins are made from tart apples or the peels of citrus fruit, both of which contain high amounts of natural pectin. Packaged pectin is available in both powdered and liquid forms; these are made differently, so are not interchangeable in recipes. Powdered and liquid pectins require different proportions of fruit, sugar, and acid in order to set. Be sure to use the specific type of pectin and package size called for in the recipe.

Using commercial pectins to make soft spreads like jams, jellies, and marmalades has several advantages. Instead of needing to use a significant amount of underripe fruit in spreads, commercial pectin allows you to use fully ripe fruit with the best flavor. The amount of cooking time is also significantly reduced, so the fruit retains a stronger flavor. Pectin allows you to make spreads with any fruit combination of varying pectin levels. Additionally, the same amount of fruit will produce a higher yield of finished spread with commercial pectin because the fruit doesn't need to cook down as much in order to set.

## Acid

Acid plays several important roles in canning. First, it helps inhibit bacterial growth in canned products during storage, which can happen if the acid level is too low. The correct acidity level is essential to ensuring safe water bath processing and storage for canned goods that are high in acid, such as jams, jellies, fruits, and pickles. Products that have low acid levels, such as vegetables, must be processed in a pressure canner to make them safe for shelf storage. Reducing the amount of acid may make the preserve unsafe for shelf-storage after processing, so always follow the recipe's specified amount of acid. Lemon juice and vinegar are the two most common types of acid used in canning recipes.

A sufficient amount of acid, in the correct ratio to the fruit, sugar, and pectin, must be present for a soft spread to gel or set. If there is too little acid, the spread will remain thin and runny. If there is too much acid, the spread will set up firmer and, during storage, some liquid may separate from the gel, a process known as syneresis, or "weeping." Weeping is evident by a thin puddle of liquid on the top surface of the spread in the jar or a layer of liquid between the side of the jar and the spread.

### ✻ LEMON JUICE ✻

For fruits that don't have enough natural acid to set the spread, like ripe peaches, the acid is usually provided by freshly squeezed lemon juice. A small amount of freshly squeezed lemon juice is added to some spread recipes to enhance the flavor of the fruit and also to help protect the color of lighter fruits and prevent them from darkening during storage. Freshly squeezed lime juice can also be used to raise the acidity level of some fruit mixtures to improve the texture and brighten the flavor of the jam or other spread. If a recipe calls for bottled lemon juice or lime juice, do not substitute fresh juice. Bottled lemon and lime juice have a consistent acidity level needed to safely can some recipes containing low-acid fruits, such as tomatoes and figs.

### ✻ VINEGAR ✻

Vinegar is used in making pickles and relishes to raise the acidity level to a level high enough to permit processing in a water bath canner. Only commercially prepared vinegars with a minimum acidity level of 5% should be used for canning; check the ingredient statement on the bottle label for the acidity level. White vinegar, cider vinegar, or wine vinegar may be used, depending on the recipe and the desired result. Commercially made herb and fruit vinegars may overpower the flavor of the produce and should be used cautiously. Homemade vinegars have an unknown acidity content and shouldn't be used in canning recipes.

## Herbs

Fresh herbs add a wonderful aromatic flavor to many types of preserves, from savory soft spreads to sauces and pickles. Fresh herbs have a stronger flavor than dried herbs. Choose young, tender fresh herbs with dark green color and undamaged leaves. For the strongest flavor, prepare the herbs just before you are ready to use them.

## Nuts and Dried Fruits

A variety of nuts and some dried fruits, such as raisins, currants, cranberries, and apricots, can be used to make conserves, which are fruit spreads containing nuts and usually dried fruit and are similar in texture to jams. Coconut is a popular addition to spreads with a tropical flair. Nuts used in spreads need to be very fresh. Stale or rancid nuts will give the conserve an unpleasant flavor. Always taste nuts before using them to make sure they are fresh. Nuts may be toasted to bring out their flavor and to accentuate their crunchy texture.

### ADDING BUTTER TO PRESERVES

Unsalted butter may be added to jams, marmalades, preserves, and conserves to help reduce the amount of foaming that occurs when the fruit mixture boils. This reduces the time spent skimming foam from the top of the jam in the pot before ladling it into the jars. Butter can cause jellies to turn cloudy, so it is not recommended that butter be added to juice mixtures when making jellies.

# * Canning * Equipment

Using the appropriate type and size of home canning equipment, including jars and lids, water bath and pressure canners, pots and pans, and utensils, will help ensure that you produce beautiful, delicious, and safe canned foods.

# Home Canning Jars and Lids

Modern canning jars with two-piece lids make home canning safe and easy. Canning jars are sold in boxes of a dozen jars that also include the lids and screw bands, and come in a variety of sizes and shapes with both standard and wide-mouth jar openings.

Old-fashioned canning jars sealed with rubber-like gaskets and screw-on one-piece lids are no longer considered safe for home canning, and the United States Department of Agriculture (USDA) does not endorse their continued use. This also applies to jars with wire-bail-attached glass lids and rubber seals; these types of jars should not be used for home canning. Newer one-piece canning lids also are available, but their use is not currently endorsed by the USDA.

## ✻ CANNING JARS ✻

USDA-approved home canning jars are made of molded heat-tempered glass and are the only containers currently recommended for safe home canning. The jars have a wide rim and screw threads that are designed to work with two-piece metal vacuum lids and screw bands.

Don't use any jars that are not specifically manufactured for home canning, including mayonnaise jars, commercial jam and jelly jars, fruit jars, condiment jars, peanut butter jars, and baby food jars, even if home canning lids and rings appear to fit them. Commercial jars are not heat-tempered like home canning jars, nor are they sturdy enough to stand up to heat processing in a water bath or pressure canner.

Jars manufactured specifically for freezer canning should not be used for canning preserves that will be processed in a water bath canner or pressure canner. Freezer jars are not tempered to withstand the high heat in the canner and may shatter during processing.

## ✻ CANNING LIDS AND SCREW BANDS ✻

The lid closures for canning jars consist of two pieces—a flat metal lid and a metal screw band. After the jars are filled, the lid is applied and the band is screwed on to hold the lid in place during processing in a water bath or pressure canner.

The underside of the metal lid has a protective food-safe coating that won't react with the acids in canned foods. The flat metal lids are designed for one-time use only and cannot be reused. A new lid must be used each time you seal a jar.

The screw band is designed to hold the lid firmly in place during processing and until the jar cools and the lid compound forms a solid seal between the lid and jar rim. After the jars have cooled completely, the screw bands should be removed for storage. It is important to use lids and screw bands made by the same manufacturer as the canning jars to ensure a proper fit and tight seal. Screw bands can be reused if they are in good condition and not rusty.

# Water Bath Canner

A water bath canner, also called a boiling water canner, is an essential piece of equipment for canning high-acid preserves, such as jams, pickles, and most fruits. It is used to process and seal jars after they have been filled and the lids applied. Years ago, water bath processing of filled jars was optional, but that is no longer the case for safety reasons and is now required when canning any high-acid food.

To make the jar contents safe for storage, the jars need to be heated in boiling water for a specified amount of time. During processing, the contents reach an internal temperature high enough to kill any potential bacteria that could cause contamination. Water bath processing will also deactivate enzymes, molds, and yeasts that could cause the preserves to deteriorate over time. To learn how to process high-acid foods in a water bath canner, see p. 24.

A water bath canner consists of a large stockpot with a lid and a rack in the bottom to hold the jars. The rack allows the hot water to circulate around and under the jars so the contents will heat evenly. You can either purchase a water bath canner specially made for the job or you can put one together yourself. Commercially made canners have racks designed to hold a certain number of jars. I find these racks awkward to use, so instead of purchasing a water bath canner, I have assembled my own. I use a 20-quart stainless steel stockpot with a glass lid and a round wire cake cooling rack in the bottom.

If you want to assemble your own water bath canner, you will need a large stockpot, preferably stainless steel, with a tight-fitting lid. It needs to be deep enough to allow for a rack in the bottom, plus the height of the jars, 1 to 2 inches of water above the top of the jars, plus another 1½ to 2 inches of height to keep the water from boiling over.

# Pressure Canner

A pressure canner is a piece of equipment specifically designed to process low-acid canned foods and seal the jars for safe storage. During processing, pressurized steam inside the canner brings the contents of the jars up to a temperature high enough to kill any bacteria spores that may be in the food.

The canner consists of a large, heavy-duty stainless steel pot with a locking lid that is clamped down to create a tight seal. A rack in the bottom of the pot securely holds and separates the jars during processing. A gauge measures the pressure inside the canner so the pressure can be maintained and adjusted as the jars are processed.

There are two basic types of pressure canners available for home canning: weighted-gauge canners and dial-gauge canners. Both work equally well for processing low-acid foods. Carefully read and follow the manufacturer's instructions that come with the canner.

Pressure canners should not be confused with pressure cookers—they are not the same piece of equipment and are not interchangeable. The internal pressure cannot be accurately regulated in a pressure cooker. Only a pressure canner specifically designed for home canning can be used to safely process low-acid foods.

## Pots and Pans

A large stockpot, preferably 8 quarts, is needed for preparing many types of preserves. This size allows enough room for cooking the preserves without boiling over and enough surface area to permit the proper evaporation of some of the liquid when making jams and soft spreads. The pot should be made of heavy-gauge stainless steel with a thick bottom and a tight-fitting lid. Stainless steel is a nonreactive material, so it is an excellent choice for making all kinds of canned foods. Some metals, such as aluminum, can have a chemical reaction with the acid in some fruits and other acidic ingredients, such as lemon juice and vinegar. A heavy pot will distribute the heat evenly and prevent hot spots that can cause the preserves to burn during cooking.

A small stainless steel saucepan is ideal for heating the canning jar lids and keeping them hot until you are ready to cover and seal the jars.

## Other Canning Tools

Using the appropriate types of measuring cups is crucial to successful canning. Standard glass liquid measuring cups work well for measuring fruit, vegetables, juice, vinegar, water, and other liquid ingredients. A set of plastic or metal dry measuring cups, in graduated sizes, with flat rims are best for measuring sugar and other dry ingredients. The top of this type of measuring cup is flat so that you can use a straight knife to level the ingredient even with the top edge to get an exact measure. A set of measuring spoons in graduated sizes is important for measuring small quantities of ingredients.

In addition to standard kitchen utensils, a few specific canning tools will make preparing and processing canned foods much easier and faster: a canning funnel, a lid wand with a magnet on one end, kitchen tongs, a jar lifter, an accurate kitchen timer, a citrus zester, a food mill (to remove seeds and skins), cheesecloth or a jelly bag with a stand, and a plastic knife or chopstick (to coax air bubbles out of jars before processing).

# * Canning * Techniques

Creating attractive, delicious canned goods with award-winning quality doesn't happen by accident. Skilled home canners follow some important preparation methods to produce outstanding preserves. These techniques can be mastered easily by home canners of any experience and skill level.

## Review the Recipe and Assemble Ingredients and Equipment

The first step in successful canning is to review the recipe. Be sure you understand the canning procedures and that you have all of the ingredients and equipment on hand and ready to use.

## Prepare Jars, Lids, and Screw Bands

Canning jars, lids, and screw bands require some basic preparation before being used. Preparing these items correctly will help form a strong seal between the lid and the jar rim.

### ❊ INSPECTING JARS, LIDS, AND SCREW BANDS ❊

Inspect all canning jars, lids, and screw bands for any visible signs of damage. Check the jars for scratches, cracks, or bubbles in the glass or any other flaws that may weaken the jars and cause them to break during processing. Run your finger around the rim of the jars and feel for any nicks, chips, rough spots, or uneven rims that will prevent the lids from properly sealing to the jar rims and discard any damaged items.

Always use new flat lids specifically designed for canning. Examine the lids to make sure they are not scratched, dinged, or warped, and that the food-safe coating on the underside of the lid isn't damaged. Scratches can rust during storage, and warped or bent lids won't seal properly. Check that the sealing compound around the edge of the lid is applied evenly and that there are no gaps or thin spots. Any gap in the sealing compound will prevent a tight seal and can cause the seal to fail during storage.

The screw bands can be reused if they are in good condition, but bands with any rust or corrosion should be discarded. Warped or dented bands shouldn't be used as they may not hold the lids securely on the jars during processing and cooling.

### ❊ WASHING AND HEATING JARS ❊

Canning jars need to be washed before each use. I like to wash my canning jars in the dishwasher because the dishwasher washes, rinses, dries, and heats the jars in one process, leaving me free to get the rest of the canning equipment ready and prepare and measure the ingredients. Keep the dishwasher door shut and locked to keep the jars hot until you need them to reduce the chance of the jars breaking when they're filled with hot preserves. If your dishwasher has a plate-warming feature, use it to keep jars hot while making several batches of preserves.

You can also wash the jars by hand in hot, soapy water and then rinse them well under hot running water to remove all of the soap. Hand-washed jars should be submerged in a pot of hot water to keep them hot until ready to use to reduce the chance of the jars breaking when filled with hot preserves.

Jars that will be processed for 10 minutes or more in a water bath canner and jars that will be processed in a pressure canner after filling do not need to be sterilized after washing. However, jars that are processed by the water bath method for less than 10 minutes need sterilizing before being filled. To sterilize jars, submerge them in a pot of hot water, bring to a boil, and boil for 10 minutes, adding 1 minute of additional time for each 1,000 feet of elevation above sea level where you're processing. When ready to fill, remove one sterilized jar from the hot water, fill, wipe the jar rim, apply the lid and screw band, and then place in the water bath canner before removing the next sterilized jar from the hot water.

Home canning jars are not designed to be used with dry heat, so never use the oven or microwave to keep jars hot while waiting to be filled. The dry heat of the oven can weaken jars and significantly increase the chance of them breaking during heat processing in a water bath or pressure canner.

### ✻ WASHING AND HEATING LIDS ✻

Wash the flat lids in hot soapy water, rinse well, and drain. Place the lids in a pan of hot water and heat for 10 minutes to soften the sealing compound. When softened, the sealing compound on the lid will mold itself to the rim of the jar and form a tight seal as the jars cool after processing. Do not boil the lids—boiling will damage the sealing compound and cause the seals to fail during storage. Because of an increase in seal failures resulting from canners boiling the lids instead of heating them, one major canning lid manufacturer has recently changed their lid preparation instructions to omit the heating step. Follow the manufacturer's instructions that come with the canning lids.

### ✻ WASHING SCREW BANDS ✻

Quickly wash the screw bands in hot soapy water and rinse well. Thoroughly dry the screw bands to prevent rusting and set aside until needed.

# Prepare and Measure Ingredients

Care needs to be taken when measuring and preparing ingredients for canning. Accuracy is essential to creating quality preserves and ensuring a finished product with a balanced flavor and the proper consistency.

### ✻ PREPARING PRODUCE ✻

The preparation of the produce for canning recipes has a direct impact on the quality of the finished product. To create a great preserve, you need to use care as you handle and prepare the fruit and vegetables you will be canning.

- Use fruits and vegetables when they are in season and at the peak of ripeness. For the freshest flavor and best texture, use the produce as soon after harvest as possible.

- Fruits and vegetables should be at room temperature before preparing recipes. Cold produce may alter the cooking time and the finished texture of the preserve. The denser the produce, the longer it can take to cook when cold.

- Produce can deteriorate quickly when wet, so rinse fruits and vegetables just before you use them. Wash most produce by gently rinsing under cool running water and drain it well. Spread the produce out on paper towels or a clean kitchen towel and gently blot dry. Citrus fruits, cucumbers, and root vegetables should be lightly scrubbed with a very soft fruit or vegetable brush, then rinsed and dried.

- Prepare and measure the ingredients according to the recipe instructions. Only prepare enough produce for one canning batch or recipe at a time. The produce can deteriorate if prepared too far in advance.

- Cut fruits and vegetables into pieces that are uniform in size, shape, and thickness to give your preserves a consistent texture and attractive appearance.

## PEELING PEACHES, APRICOTS, AND TOMATOES

There are a few fruits and vegetables you should peel in order for your preserves to have the best texture. These include peaches, apricots, and tomatoes. To make short work of peeling these ingredients, slash a small X on the bottom of the fruit, then gently drop them, a few at a time, into a pan of boiling water. Let them soak in the water for 30 to 60 seconds, or until the peels on the peaches or apricots start to release or the skins on the tomatoes just start to split. Quickly remove the fruit from the boiling water with a slotted spoon and immediately plunge it into a large bowl or pan of ice water. Let the fruit sit in the ice water for 1 to 2 minutes to stop the cooking process. When the fruit is cool enough to handle, use a small sharp paring knife to remove the peel or skin.

**✻ ACCURATELY MEASURING INGREDIENTS ✻**

The accurate measurement of fruit, sugar, and other ingredients in preserves plays a key role in the outcome of the finished product. Using the correct types of measuring cups for different ingredients is very important.

For measuring ingredients such as fruits, vegetables, juice, and vinegar, use glass measuring cups that are made for measuring liquid ingredients. Level off the top of the fruit and read the markings at eye level.

For dry ingredients like sugar, use measuring cups with flat rims that are specifically designed for measuring dry ingredients. These measuring cups allow you to spoon or pour the dry ingredient into the cup and use a knife or utensil with a straight edge to scrape the excess off the top of the cup to get an accurate measurement.

Use graduated measuring spoons for measuring small portions of both liquid and dry ingredients. Small glass measuring glasses may also be used for measuring small quantities of liquids.

## Filling Jars

Before filling jars, carefully remove the number of hot canning jars you need from the dishwasher and set the jars upright on a towel or heatproof cutting board on the counter. Or, using a jar lifter, remove the jars from the pot of hot water, carefully pouring the water inside the jars back into the pan, and place them upside down on a towel for a minute to drain out the remaining water. Turn the jars upright.

### PREPARING HOT AND SWEET PEPPERS

When working with chile peppers, handle the peppers with care. Chile peppers contain strong oils that can cause chemical burns on your skin, in your mouth, and in your eyes. Always wear latex, plastic, or rubber gloves when seeding and chopping hot peppers to avoid direct contact between your skin and the peppers. Do not wipe your hands across your face or rub your eyes while working with hot peppers.

The seeds and pith are the hottest part of a chile pepper. Remove them for a milder flavor and leave them in when you want more heat. The white or light-colored ribs on the inside of peppers are very fibrous and can become quite tough when cooked, affecting both the flavor and texture of a preserve. The white ribs should be removed from the peppers after seeding and before chopping.

Hot canning jars should always be placed on a paper or cloth towel, cutting board, or wire rack. If placed directly on a cold countertop, such as tile or granite, hot jars can break from the sudden change in temperature to the bottom of the jar. When jars are filled with hot preserves, the temperature contrast between the heat of the preserves and the cold of the countertop can also cause jars to break.

A wide-mouth funnel made specifically for canning is an indispensable tool for filling canning jars. Set the funnel in the top of a jar and use a ladle to transfer the hot preserves from the pan to the jar, leaving the correct headspace. For raw pack preserves, arrange the fruit or vegetables in the jar, then place the funnel in the jar and ladle the hot covering liquid into the jars to the appropriate height.

Keep the ladle close to the funnel and fill the jars quickly to prevent air bubbles from forming and becoming trapped in the jars as you fill them. Small air bubbles trapped in jars of spreads and relishes are a cosmetic issue. However, large air bubbles are a problem because they can create air pockets where bacteria could grow. These large air bubbles should be removed before closing the jar.

To remove trapped air bubbles, slide a thin-bladed plastic knife or plastic chopstick down into the jar to create a path for the air bubbles to rise to the surface. Be careful not to trap additional air in the jar as you remove the knife. For jars of fruits, vegetables, and pickles, after removing air bubbles, you may need to add more liquid to bring the headspace back up to the correct level.

The jar yield given in a canning recipe is an approximation and should be used as a guide when filling jars. The actual number of jars you get from a batch of preserves may vary.

### ❊ HEADSPACE ❊

Headspace is the specific amount of space, or air gap, you need to leave between the top of the preserve and the top edge of the jar. No more, no less. During processing, the contents of the jar expand and air is forced out under the lid. As the jar starts to cool, a vacuum is created inside the jar, pulling the lid tight against the rim of the jar.

It is extremely important to closely follow the headspace requirements for home canning. This is a matter of canning safety. Extensive testing has been done to determine the appropriate amount of headspace to leave inside jars to produce the best seal and make the preserves safe for shelf storage.

If too much headspace is left in the top of the jar, the air won't fully vent from the jar during processing. This will prevent a strong vacuum from forming in the jar and the lid won't pull down tightly against the jar rim to create a solid seal.

If there is too little headspace left in the jar, then some of the preserve or liquid may be forced out between the lid and the rim of the jar during processing. Any food particles trapped between the lid compound and the jar rim will result in a jar with a weak seal. These trapped food particles will create a pathway for bacteria to enter the jar, and the weakened seal will likely fail during storage.

### ❊ WIPE JAR RIMS ❊

After filling the jars, use a clean damp paper towel to remove any spilled preserves or liquid from the rim of the jar and the jar screw threads. Any food residue left on the rim of the jars may prevent a firm bond between the lid and jar rim and cause a weak seal. Drips left on the screw threads of the jar can prevent the screw band from pulling the lid down snug against the jar rim.

Never use a kitchen sponge to wipe down the jar rims. Sponges can harbor a host of bacteria that can easily be transferred to the jars and contaminate the preserves.

### ❊ APPLY LIDS AND SCREW BANDS ❊

Use a magnetic lid wand or kitchen tongs to carefully remove the heated lids, one at a time, from the pan of hot water. Center the lids on the jars with the sealing compound centered on the jar rims.

Place a screw band on each jar and screw the band down onto the jar threads. With your fingers, screw the band down until resistance is met, and then increase the pressure until the band is fingertip tight. Don't use force to tighten the screw band—overtightening can prevent the jars from venting air and forming a vacuum during heat processing, which can lead to seal failure. It can also cause the jars to break inside the canner, or while removing the jars from the canner, because of the pressure buildup inside the jars.

During processing, the compound on the flat lid will soften and form a partial seal with the rim of the canning jar. The softened compound will allow air to escape from the jar during processing, but prevent water from entering the jar. With the temperature change that occurs after the jar is removed from the canner, a vacuum will form inside the jar that will pull the lid down tight against the jar rim—you will hear the lid pop when this happens. As the jar continues to cool, the compound will harden and form a permanent seal holding the lid firmly in place. After 24 hours, when the compound has hardened and the seal is complete, the screw band should be removed from the jar to prevent rusting.

Screw bands may loosen slightly during processing. This is normal and you should never retighten the screw bands after processing. When the jars come out of the canner, the compound on the lids will be hot and very soft. If you retighten the screw band, you could force the compound out from between the lid and the jar rim. This will break the seal or result in a very weak seal, which could fail during storage.

## Making Soft Spreads

There are two basic methods for making jams, jellies, and other soft spreads—the short-boil method and the long-boil method. The two methods yield spreads with significantly different characteristics, including different flavors and textures. The short-boil method produces spreads that have a softer texture and a flavor closer to that of fresh fruit, while spreads made by the long-boil method can range from very soft to firm and have a definite cooked fruit flavor.

### ❊ SHORT-BOIL METHOD ❊

In the short-boil method, commercial packaged pectin is added to the fruit and sugar mixture to create spreads with a bright, tantalizing flavor and tender texture. The short-boil method dramatically decreases the amount of cooking time needed to make soft spreads. Soft spread recipes using commercial pectin are formulated to work with the natural pectin of fully ripe fruit. Because the fruit is cooked for a shorter period of time in short-boil spreads, the fruit retains more of its intense natural color and flavor.

There are two types of commercial packaged pectin—powdered pectin and liquid pectin. With powdered pectin, the pectin and fruit are combined first, brought to a boil, and then the sugar is added. With liquid pectin, the fruit and sugar are combined, brought to a boil, and then the pectin is added. In both cases, after all the ingredients are combined, the mixture is boiled and stirred for 1 minute and then removed from the heat. It is a quick and easy way to make spreads that yield excellent results.

### ❊ LONG-BOIL METHOD ❊

In the long-boil method, the fruit is combined with the sugar and then boiled for several minutes. Some fruits are high in natural pectin while others contain very little pectin. It is often necessary to use a high percentage of underripe fruit, which contains more pectin than ripe fruit, in order to get the spread to set. Fruits with a low pectin content require a longer cooking time as the spread gels more through a process of evaporation of juice than the pectin setting. If cooked too long, the spread can become gummy or sticky.

Because the spread must cook for a period of time over moderately high heat in order to evaporate enough liquid to help thicken the mixture, there is a greater risk that the fruit in the bottom of the pan may scorch if not closely watched. The extended cooking time can also cause the sugar to caramelize and the spread to take on a molasses-like flavor and color.

Making quality spreads with the long-boil method takes some practice and skill. Because these spreads set through a combination of evaporation of liquid and activation of pectin to create a gel, there is a tendency to overcook the spread to get it to set. The hazard of overcooking a spread is that it can set up very firm or sticky.

When cooking jams and jellies using the long-boil method, cook the fruit and sugar mixture until thick and glossy and it reaches the jellying point, also known as the setting point, of 220°F measured on a canning or candy thermometer. Watch the temperature carefully—spreads heated above 220°F can set up too firm.

### Jellying Point for Jams, Jellies, and Other Soft Spreads

When cooking soft spreads by the long-boil method, boil the mixture until it reaches the following temperature on a canning or candy thermometer for your altitude.

| Sea Level | 1,000 ft. | 2,000 ft. | 3,000 ft. | 4,000 ft. | 5,000 ft. | 6,000 ft. | 7,000 ft. | 8,000 ft. |
|---|---|---|---|---|---|---|---|---|
| 220°F | 218°F | 216°F | 214°F | 212°F | 211°F | 209°F | 207°F | 205°F |

# * Processing * Canning Jars

Even though sugar and acid act as preservatives in jars of jams, other soft spreads, fruits, pickles, relishes, and sauces, molds and bacteria can still grow inside the jars and cause these products to spoil if not properly processed. It used to be thought that filling sterilized jars with hot preserves and turning the jars upside down for a few minutes was sufficient to seal the jars and prevent mold growth. This is no longer the case. To prevent mold and bacteria growth, the USDA and the Cooperative Extension Service strongly advise that all high-acid foods be processed in a water bath canner and all low-acid foods be processed in a pressure canner to ensure the safety of the canned product.

## Heat Processing

Heat processing of home-canned foods is necessary to destroy any microorganisms that could cause the food to spoil during storage. Processing also vents air from inside the jars, which creates a vacuum and allows a tight seal to form between the lid and the jar. Processing filled jars for the correct length of time, and following approved guidelines will ensure that the product is safe to store on the shelf and maintain maximum flavor, color, and texture.

Heat processing in a water bath canner is the approved and recommended method for destroying microorganisms and sealing jars of all canned foods that are high in acid. In addition to soft spreads, this is also the method used to process jars of fruit, fruit juices, tomato products to which lemon juice or vinegar has been added to increase the acid content, pickles, and many sauces. Foods that are low in acid, such as vegetables, must be processed in a pressure canner.

### ❊ WATER BATH PROCESSING ❊

When you process filled jars of jam, fruit, and other high-acid preserves in a water bath, the jars are submerged in boiling water long enough for all the food inside the jar to reach a temperature high enough to kill any harmful bacteria, mold spores, or yeasts that may be present in the jarred food. The boiling water bath also pulls air out of the jar, creating a vacuum inside the jar and a tight seal between the lid and the jar rim, preventing any bacteria from entering the processed jar.

### ❊ PRESSURE CANNER PROCESSING ❊

Jars of vegetables and other low-acid foods must be processed in a pressure canner. During pressure canner processing, the contents of the jar are brought to a high enough temperature to kill any bacteria or other contaminants that may be present in the food. The canning process also creates a vacuum in the jars and produces a tight seal between the lid and jar. Pressure canner processing makes low-acid preserves safe for shelf storage.

## Altitude Adjustments for Heat Processing

Water boils at 212°F at sea level. As altitude increases, water boils at a lower temperature, which means it is less effective at killing bacteria. To compensate for the lower boiling point, water bath processing times need to be increased as altitude increases. When pressure canning at altitudes above 2,000 feet, you will need to increase the pounds of pressure used for safe processing.

The processing times listed in the recipes are based on an altitude of 1,000 feet or less for water bath canning and an altitude of 2,000 feet or less for pressure canning. If you live at a higher altitude, adjust your processing time as indicated on p. 22.

### Altitude Adjustments for Water Bath Processing

| ALTITUDE IN FEET | INCREASE PROCESSING TIME BY |
|---|---|
| 1,001 to 3,000 | 5 minutes |
| 3,001 to 6,000 | 10 minutes |
| 6,001 to 8,000 | 15 minutes |
| 8,001 to 10,000 | 20 minutes |

### Altitude Adjustments for Pressure Canner Processing

| ALTITUDE IN FEET | DIAL-GAUGE PRESSURE CANNER | WEIGHTED-GAUGE PRESSURE CANNER |
|---|---|---|
| Up to 2,000 | 11 pounds | 10 pounds |
| 2,001 to 4,000 | 12 pounds | 15 pounds |
| 4,001 to 6,000 | 13 pounds | 15 pounds |
| 6,001 to 8,100 | 14 pounds | 15 pounds |
| 8,001 to 10,000 | 15 pounds | 15 pounds |

## Storing Preserves

The screw bands should be removed from the jars after the jars are sealed and the contents have cooled completely. The purpose of the screw band is to hold the lid securely in place during processing. Once the jars have cooled and the lid is securely attached to the jar, the band is not needed for storage of the jars. Screw bands left on the jars may rust during storage. When giving a jar of a preserves as a gift, always put a new screw band on the jar.

To keep the jars safe during storage, it is best to place them on stable shelves with a raised front rail or pack the jars in sturdy boxes. Never stack canning jars on top of each other for storage. The weight of the top jar pressing down on the lid of the bottom jar can cause the seal to fail on the lower jar.

Jars of preserves should be stored in a cool, dark, dry location to preserve the color, flavor, and texture of the canned item. If left in a warm environment, canned foods can deteriorate faster and lose their intense flavor. Exposure to light for an extended period of time speeds up oxidation and can cause the color, as well as the flavor, to fade. Moist locations can cause the lids to rust. Locations that are both warm and moist can damage the seal and encourage the growth of mold.

The ideal temperature range for storing jars of home-canned foods, and the one recommended by the USDA, is between 50°F and 70°F. Jars stored at temperatures higher than 70°F may deteriorate faster. If you are fortunate to have a basement or cellar, these are ideal locations for storing home-canned preserves. Other good locations for storing jar boxes include the back of a pantry, on the floor or lower shelves of an interior closet, or under a bed.

For the best overall quality, use home-canned foods within a year after canning. While a well-canned preserve should remain safe to eat as long as the jar seal remains intact and the product shows no visible signs of spoilage, the appearance and flavor of the food will deteriorate over time.

## Unsafe Canning Methods

There are several old-fashioned, outdated home canning methods that used to be considered acceptable canning practice but have been scientifically proven to be unsafe. Unfortunately, these unsafe methods are still being used today by some home canners. Any preserve made using these methods should be considered at high risk for contamination or spoilage and unsafe to eat.

### ✻ OPEN-KETTLE METHOD ✻

The theory behind open-kettle canning, also known as the inversion method, was that any bacteria or organisms in the food were killed when the mixture was boiled. The preserve was poured into sterilized jars, the rims wiped down, and a lid and screw band applied. The jars were then inverted (turned upside down) for 5 to 10 minutes. When the jars were turned back upright, the lid would pull down as a vacuum was created inside the jar. Because the preserve was considered sterile, it was thought that contaminants would not grow inside the jar.

In actuality, open-kettle canning carries many serious health risks. Bacteria and mold spores can enter the jar or contaminate the preserve before the jar is closed.

Even if the jars appear to seal by inversion, the seals will be weak and likely to fail during storage. The temperature of the food inside the jar is rarely hot enough to kill any contaminants that may have entered the jar while it was being filled and closed. In addition, the air has not been exhausted from inside the jars to create a strong vacuum and the jar retains enough oxygen to allow the growth of mold or other contaminants. Inverting the jars is not an acceptable substitute for water bath processing of high-acid foods.

*Continued on p. 27.*

# STEP-BY-STEP WATER BATH CANNING GUIDE

**1.** Wash canning jars and keep hot until ready to use.

**2.** Wash the lids and screw bands in hot, soapy water and rinse well. Dry thoroughly and set aside.

**3.** Fill the water bath canner pot two-thirds full of water. Place on the stovetop, cover, and heat over medium-high heat.

**4.** Prepare and measure the ingredients according to the recipe.

**5.** Place the flat lids in a small pan of hot water. Cover and keep the lids hot off the heat for 10 minutes or until ready to use. Do not boil the lids. **(A, p. 25)**

**6.** Prepare and cook the preserves according to the recipe.

**7.** Place the hot jars upright on a towel or a heatproof cutting board.

**8.** Fill the jars, leaving the headspace indicated in the recipe. **(B, p. 25)**

**9.** Wipe the jar rims and threads with a clean, damp paper towel.

**10.** Place the hot lids on the jars and apply the screw bands until fingertip-tight. Do not overtighten the bands. **(C, p. 25)**

**11.** Position the rack in the water bath canner.

**12.** Using a jar lifter, carefully load the jars into the canner. Make sure the jars do not touch the sides of the canner and leave 1 inch of space between the jars. Make sure the water level is at least 1 to 2 inches above the tops of the jars. Add more hot water, if necessary. **(D and E, p. 25)**

**13.** Cover the canner and bring the water to a boil over high heat. Reduce the heat to maintain a gentle boil during processing.

**14.** Start the timer after the water reaches a boil. Check the canner periodically to make sure the water is still boiling. If the boiling stops, return the water to a boil, reset the timer for the full amount of time, and resume processing the jars. Adjust the processing time for altitudes above 1,000 feet (see p. 22).

**15.** When the processing time is complete, turn off the heat and remove the lid from the canner.

**16.** Using a jar lifter, remove the jars from the canner and set the jars on a cooling rack or cloth towel, spacing at least 1 inch apart. Do not retighten the screw bands. Cool, undisturbed, for 12 to 24 hours to allow the seals to set. **(F, p. 25)**

**17.** Check the seals on the cooled jars by pressing down in the center of each lid. If the lid is depressed and does not move when pressed, the jar is sealed. Unsealed jars should be stored in the refrigerator and the contents used within a few days. **(G, p. 25)**

**18.** Remove the screw bands. Keeping the jars upright, gently wash in warm soapy water, rinse well, and dry thoroughly. Label if desired. **(H and I, p. 25)**

A

B

C

D

E

F

G

H

I

# STEP-BY-STEP PRESSURE CANNING GUIDE

**1.** Wash canning jars and keep hot until ready to use.

**2.** Wash the lids and screw bands in hot, soapy water and rinse well. Dry thoroughly and set aside.

**3.** Position the rack in the pressure canner. Fill a dial-gauge canner with 3 inches of water or a weighted-gauge canner with 5 inches of water, or the amount recommended by the manufacturer. Place on the stovetop and start heating over low heat.

**4.** Prepare and measure the ingredients according to the recipe.

**5.** Place the flat lids in a small pan of hot water. Cover and keep the lids hot off the heat for 10 minutes until ready to use. Do not boil the lids. **(A, p. 25)**

**6.** Prepare and cook the preserves according to the recipe.

**7.** Place the hot jars upright on a towel or a heatproof cutting board.

**8.** Fill the jars, leaving the headspace indicated in the recipe. **(B, p. 25)**

**9.** Wipe the jar rims and threads with a clean, damp paper towel.

**10.** Place the hot lids on the jars, and apply the screw bands until fingertip-tight. Do not overtighten the bands. **(C, p. 25)**

**11.** Using a jar lifter, carefully load the jars into the canner. Make sure the jars do not touch the sides of the canner and leave 1 inch of space between the jars. **(D and E, p. 25)**

**12.** Place the lid on the canner and lock it in place. For a dial-gauge canner, leave the petcock open. For a weighted-gauge canner, leave the weighted gauge off the vent. Increase the heat to medium high. When steam begins to escape from the petcock or vent, set a timer for 10 minutes.

**13.** After the canner has vented for 10 minutes, close the petcock or place the weighted gauge on the vent. It will take about 5 minutes for the canner to come up to pressure.

**14.** Start the timer when the canner reaches the processing pressure indicated in the recipe. Adjust the heat as needed to maintain the correct pressure, or slightly above, for the entire processing time. Adjust the processing time for altitudes above 2,000 feet (see p. 22).

**15.** When the processing time is complete, turn off the heat. Let the canner cool and depressurize until the gauge reads 0 before opening the petcock or removing the weighted gauge from the vent. Let the canner vent steam for 2 minutes before unlocking and removing the lid from the canner. Allow the jars to cool in the canner for 5 minutes.

**16.** To remove jars, check seals, and remove screw bands, refer to steps 16-18 on p. 24.

*Unsafe Canning Methods, continued from p. 23.*

### ❊ INVERTING JARS AFTER PROCESSING ❊

Some home canners still cannot let go of the notion that jars need to be inverted, even after the jars have been water bath processed. This is a dangerous practice. Inverting jars after water bath processing can weaken the seal and allow the preserve to seep between the jar and lid. Bacteria and mold can then enter and grow inside the jar, contaminating the contents.

### ❊ OTHER UNSAFE CANNING METHODS ❊

Other unsafe and outdated methods of canning include attempting to process and seal the filled jars in the oven, microwave, or dishwasher. There is no way to control the temperature of the contents of the jars with these hazardous methods. There is also a high risk of the jars shattering. None of these methods will properly seal jars and all are considered unsafe and very dangerous.

## A Final Word on Food Safety

Bacteria and other microorganisms can be found in all foods and live on surfaces in your kitchen. It is important to eliminate as many of these contaminants as possible when preparing home-canned foods. Store-bought and home-grown fruits and vegetables should be rinsed in cool clear water before canning. Always wash your hands before handling food, and make sure that your cooking utensils and work surfaces are clean.

You can't take shortcuts or skip steps when canning and expect to produce a safe product. Follow the instructions and approved safety procedures and you will create beautiful, delicious, and safe-to-eat preserved foods you can enjoy throughout the year and will be proud to share with family and friends.

# * Jams, Jellies, Syrups & Marmalades *

Well-made homemade preserves have a vibrant color and intense flavor that can't be matched by any store-bought variety. The easiest to prepare, jams are made from chopped and crushed fruit that is cooked with sugar until the fruit becomes translucent. Jellies are transparent, jewel-like spreads made from the extracted juice of the fruit. Syrups can turn everyday meals and desserts into special treats. Marmalades have fruit tantalizingly suspended in a tender, shimmery jelly.

## Preparing Fruit for Jams

Preparing fruit for making jam is simple and straightforward. Gently rinse the fruit under cool running water to remove any dirt or dust. Spread it out on paper towels or clean kitchen towels in a single layer and gently blot the fruit dry. Wash berries just before using and handle them carefully as they are fragile and damage easily. Sturdier fruits, such as apples and citrus, can sit at room temperature for a while after washing without deteriorating. Peel and pit stone fruits, core and peel apples and pears, and hull or stem berries. Fruit should always be peeled because the peels or skins become tough and gummy when cooked.

Cut the peeled fruit into small pieces and then gently crush with a potato or vegetable masher, one layer at a time to ensure the fruit is evenly crushed, in a flat-bottomed pan or bowl. You want to end up with lots of smaller crushed pieces of fruit. Transfer the fruit to a measuring cup before adding more fruit and crushing the next layer. Avoid getting carried away with the masher—you do not want to purée the fruit. Puréeing the fruit releases too much juice and will make the spread soft and runny. The jam also will be more likely to fail to set. The exception to puréeing is when making a seedless berry jam, where the process of removing the seeds creates a smooth berry pulp.

## Extracting Juice for Jellies and Syrups

The process of making jelly is similar to that of jam, except that jelly-making involves two processes: one to extract the juice from the fruit and the second to transform the juice into jelly. The fruit used to make jellies should be peeled, pitted, and crushed or finely chopped. The peels can give the extracted juice a bitter or earthy taste, so it's best to remove them before juicing the fruit. Never purée fruit when making jellies—doing so blends the fruit pulp and juice together rather than allowing the juice to separate from the fruit pulp. Jellies made from puréed fruits will be very cloudy.

To extract the juice for jellies or syrups, gently cook the fruit until very soft to release the juice. Strain the fruit and juice through a fine-mesh sieve lined with damp, fine-knit cheesecloth or in a damp jelly bag placed over a large bowl. This process can take time and should not be rushed—the juice needs to drain slowly to prevent it from turning cloudy. If you force the juice through the cheesecloth or squeeze the jelly bag, the juice will retain tiny pieces of fruit pulp and cause the finished jelly to be opaque and cloudy instead of crystal clear. To speed the process, you can strain the fruit mixture through a fine-mesh sieve first to remove the bulk of the fruit pulp from the juice before straining through the cheesecloth. If the cheesecloth fibers become clogged with pulp, pour the unstrained fruit mixture into a container, rinse the cheesecloth or jelly bag to clean the fabric, and resume the straining process through the cleaned fabric.

Pectin is frequently added to jelly recipes because few fruit juices contain enough natural pectin to create a gel on their own. The addition of pectin also substantially reduces the cooking time, which means the jelly will have a fresher flavor closer to that of the natural flavor of the fruit.

## Making Marmalades

A marmalade is a sweet and tangy spread made from citrus fruit. It normally contains both small chopped pieces of citrus along with thin strips of the colored outer peel of the citrus. Both the fruit and peel are evenly suspended in a shimmering, translucent jelly that will hold its shape and mound up in a spoon. The texture of marmalade is similar to that of jam. Marmalades can be made with a variety of citrus fruits, a combination of two or more citrus fruits, and by using both citrus and other fruits.

There are two keys to making an exceptional marmalade. The first is to use only the outer colored portion of the peel of the citrus, known as the zest. The white portion of the peel, called the pith, is very fibrous and will give the finished marmalade a bitter, unpleasant flavor. Zest should be cut into very thin strips, not thick strips or large chunks. Large strips of cooked peel can be very tough and difficult to chew and will detract from the texture of the spread. I use a handheld zesting tool to quickly and easily remove several thin, uniform strips of zest from the citrus fruit with each stroke. A vegetable peeler can be used to remove only the outer colored portion of the peel and then the zest can be sliced very thin with a sharp knife.

The second step to creating a great marmalade is to cut away the fibrous membrane that surrounds each citrus fruit section. The white membrane is tough and chewy, and becomes even tougher when cooked. It detracts from both the flavor and texture of the marmalade. Although it is more work, taking the time to remove the membrane from the sections before chopping the fruit will produce a marmalade with an intense citrus flavor and tender texture. It is well worth the effort.

To separate the fruit sections from the membrane, after removing the zest, slice the top and bottom off of the citrus. Place the citrus on a cutting board, cut side down, and use a sharp knife to cut the peel from the citrus in thick strips. Be sure to remove all of the white pith from the outside of the citrus. Holding the peeled citrus in your hand, carefully use a small paring knife to cut between the citrus sections and the membrane. Discard the membrane, remove any seeds from the sections, and chop the citrus sections.

# Simple Fruit Jam

CONTRIBUTORS: SARA AND MICHAEL LAUSMANN, OREGON

MAKES ABOUT EIGHT 8-OUNCE JARS

**4 cups crushed or puréed fresh fruit or berries**

**4 cups granulated sugar**

**1 box (2 ounces) powdered pectin**

**½ tablespoon freshly squeezed lemon juice**

**½ teaspoon unsalted butter (optional)**

Sara affectionately calls this her jam "formula" rather than her jam recipe. It can be easily adjusted for the amount of fruit you have, and it works well with any fruit—strawberries, apricots, raspberries, or whatever you have on hand. The beauty and flavor are in its simplicity and the freshness of the fruit.

1. In an 8-quart stainless steel stockpot, combine the fruit and sugar. Bring the mixture to a boil over medium heat, stirring constantly.
2. Stir in the pectin, lemon juice, and butter, if using. Return the mixture to a full rolling boil, stirring constantly. Boil for 1 minute, stirring constantly. Remove the pot from the heat and skim off any foam.
3. Ladle the jam into hot jars, leaving ¼-inch headspace. Remove any air bubbles. Wipe the jar rims and threads with a clean, damp paper towel. Apply hot lids and screw bands.
4. Process 4-ounce, 8-ounce, and pint jars in a water bath canner for 10 minutes (see p. 24 for instructions). Remove from the water bath canner and let cool for 12 to 24 hours. Check the seals and remove the screw bands. Store jars in a cool, dry, dark place for up to 1 year.

**DID YOU KNOW?**

In 1790, French chemist Louis Nicolas Vanquelin discovered a chemical in apple cider vinegar with gelatinous properties. This substance was pectin. In 1825, Henri Braconnot, a French chemist and pharmacist, was the first person to isolate and describe pectin, although the action of pectin to thicken jams and marmalades had been known for many years. It wouldn't be until the 20th century before the structure and working properties of pectin were fully identified.

# Pear Lime Jam

CONTRIBUTOR: LINDA J. AMENDT, CALIFORNIA

**MAKES ABOUT SIX 8-OUNCE JARS**

**5 cups granulated sugar**

**1 box (1.75 ounces) powdered pectin**

**$4\frac{1}{2}$ cups peeled, cored, chopped, and lightly crushed Bartlett pears (about $4\frac{1}{2}$ pounds pears)**

**3 tablespoons freshly squeezed lime juice**

**1 tablespoon finely grated lime zest**

**$\frac{1}{2}$ teaspoon unsalted butter (optional)**

When she received a big box of ripe Bartlett pears as a thank-you gift from a friend, Linda decided to make pear jam. But she didn't have any lemons at the time, only limes. That was a lucky turn of events—the lime juice and zest add a bright zing and complement the pear flavor, creating a delightful jam. This is now her favorite pear jam recipe.

1. In a small bowl, combine $\frac{1}{4}$ cup of the sugar with the pectin until thoroughly blended.

2. In an 8-quart stainless steel stockpot, combine the pears, lime juice, and lime zest. Stir in the pectin mixture and add the butter, if using. Bring the mixture to a full rolling boil over medium-high heat, stirring constantly.

3. Add the remaining sugar and stir until completely dissolved. Return the mixture to a full rolling boil, stirring constantly. Boil for 1 minute, stirring constantly.

4. Remove the pot from the heat and skim off any foam. Let the jam cool in the pot for 5 minutes, stirring occasionally.

5. Ladle the jam into hot jars, leaving $\frac{1}{4}$-inch headspace. Remove any air bubbles. Wipe the jar rims and threads with a clean, damp paper towel. Apply hot lids and screw bands.

6. Process 4-ounce, 8-ounce, and pint jars in a water bath canner for 10 minutes (see p. 24 for instructions). Remove from the water bath canner and let cool for 12 to 24 hours. Check the seals and remove the screw bands. Store jars in a cool, dry, dark place for up to 1 year.

# Wine Jelly

CONTRIBUTOR: LINDA J. AMENDT, CALIFORNIA

MAKES ABOUT SEVEN 8-OUNCE JARS

**4 cups wine**

**6 cups granulated sugar**

**2 pouches (3 ounces each) liquid pectin**

Linda likes to use Cabernet Sauvignon, Chardonnay, or White Zinfandel wine to make this jelly. Her dad's favorite was the Cabernet Sauvignon jelly. Any full-bodied wine works well in this jelly. The key is to not let the wine boil; otherwise, the jelly may take on an unpleasant flavor.

1. In an 8-quart stainless steel stockpot, combine the wine and sugar. Heat the wine over medium heat to just below simmering, stirring constantly until the sugar is completely dissolved. Tiny bubbles will form on the bottom of the pan, but not rise to the surface. Do not allow the wine to boil. Remove the pot from the heat.

2. Stir in the entire contents of both pectin pouches until thoroughly combined. Quickly skim off any foam.

3. Immediately ladle the jelly into hot jars, leaving ¼-inch headspace. Wipe the jar rims and threads with a clean, damp paper towel. Apply hot lids and screw bands.

4. Process 4-ounce, 8-ounce, and pint jars in a water bath canner for 10 minutes (see p. 24 for instructions). Remove from the water bath canner and let cool for 12 to 24 hours. Check the seals and remove the screw bands. Store jars in a cool, dry, dark place for up to 1 year.

# Berry Syrup

CONTRIBUTOR: SHIRLEY ROSENBERG, UTAH

MAKES 3 TO 4 PINT JARS

**2 quarts fresh or thawed frozen whole berries, crushed**

**6¾ cups granulated sugar**

**¼ teaspoon unsalted butter (optional)**

**NOTE:**

Jars or bottles with wire-bail-attached glass lids and rubber seals are not endorsed for canning use by the USDA. Contents should be refrigerated and used within a few days.

This syrup is delicious made from any unsweetened berry juice. Try raspberry, blackberry, or blueberry. In addition to a variety of berry syrups, Shirley also has made spiced apple syrup and spiced pear syrup. This recipe is as versatile as your imagination and taste buds!

1. In a 4-quart stainless steel stockpot, bring the crushed berries to a boil over medium-high heat, stirring frequently. Reduce the heat and simmer, stirring frequently, until the berries are very soft, about 10 minutes. Remove the pot from the heat and let cool for a few minutes. Strain the mixture through a fine-mesh sieve to separate the juice from the pulp. Discard the pulp. For a clearer syrup, line the sieve with a few layers of damp fine-knit cheesecloth and strain the juice again. Measure out 5 cups of berry juice.

2. Pour the berry juice into an 8-quart stainless steel stockpot. Stir in the sugar and add the butter, if using. Bring the mixture to a boil over medium-high heat, stirring constantly, until the sugar is completely dissolved. Reduce the heat to medium and boil, stirring frequently, until the syrup is thickened, 5 to 8 minutes. The longer the mixture boils, the thicker the syrup will be. Remove the pot from the heat.

3. Ladle the syrup into hot jars, leaving ½-inch headspace. Remove any air bubbles. Wipe the jar rims and threads with a clean, damp paper towel. Apply hot lids and screw bands.

4. Process 8-ounce and pint jars in a water bath canner for 10 minutes (see p. 24 for instructions). Remove from the water bath canner and let cool for 12 to 24 hours. Check the seals and remove the screw bands. Store jars in a cool, dry, dark place for up to 1 year.

**TIP**

For a chunky syrup, include some of the fruit pulp in the juice.

# Red Onion Marmalade

CONTRIBUTOR: BRENDA BUSTILLOS, TEXAS

MAKES ABOUT FOUR TO FIVE 8-OUNCE JARS

**1½ cups halved and thinly sliced red onions (about 2 medium onions)**

**½ cup finely chopped dried cranberries**

**¼ cup lightly packed brown sugar**

**¼ cup cider vinegar**

**2 teaspoons finely grated orange zest**

**2½ cups unsweetened apple juice**

**1 box (1.75 ounces) powdered pectin**

**3½ cups granulated sugar**

**SERVING SUGGESTION**

This marmalade makes a great accompaniment or glaze for baked ham or smoked pork ribs, and also makes a great filling for a freshly baked bread product.

This special marmalade recipe was a big hit when Brenda used it to make a sweet bread for the Texas State Fair Fleischmann's® Yeast Bake for a Cure special contest. Her Red Onion Apricot Braid won first prize and the marmalade was the key ingredient!

1. In a large skillet, over medium heat, combine the red onions, cranberries, brown sugar, and vinegar. Cook, stirring constantly, until the onions are translucent, about 10 minutes. Do not let them brown.

2. In an 8-quart stainless steel stockpot, combine the cooked onion mixture, orange zest, and apple juice. Stir in the pectin. Bring the mixture to a full rolling boil over medium-high heat, stirring constantly.

3. Add the sugar and stir constantly until completely dissolved. Return the mixture to a full rolling boil, stirring constantly. Boil for 1 minute, stirring constantly.

4. Ladle the marmalade into hot jars, leaving ¼-inch headspace. Remove any air bubbles. Wipe the jar rims and threads with a clean, damp paper towel. Apply hot lids and screw bands.

5. Process 4-ounce, 8-ounce, and pint jars in a water bath canner for 10 minutes (see p. 24 for instructions). Remove from the water bath canner and let cool for 12 to 24 hours. Check the seals and remove the screw bands. Store jars in a cool, dry, dark place for up to 1 year.

# * Pickles, Relishes, Sauces & Salsas *

Crispy, crunchy pickles are canning staples. But they don't happen by accident. Selecting quality produce and careful processing will yield high-quality results. Relishes can be prepared from a variety of vegetables and can range in flavor from sweet to very hot, depending on your preference and the tastes of your family. When you have a variety of homemade sauces and salsas on the shelf, a delicious meal is never far away.

## Canning Pickles and Relishes

Produce starts to deteriorate quickly, so it is important to use it as soon after harvest as possible. Pickling cucumbers and squash, like zucchini, can develop hollow centers if too many days pass between harvest and canning. If these vegetables are left whole, the hollow centers can trap air pockets that may cause the pickles to float in the jars and harbor bacteria that may not be killed during processing.

Select firm, fresh, unblemished produce. While most cucumber pickles are best made with pickling cucumbers, relishes are more forgiving, and many can be made with standard slicing cucumbers. Just be sure to remove any large seeds before chopping or grinding the cucumbers.

## Preparing Vegetables

Rinse vegetables under cool running water and scrub gently with a soft brush to remove all dirt and sand. Be careful not to scrub too hard and damage the produce. Cut a thin slice off the blossom end of cucumbers and squash to remove the blossom scar. For root vegetables, such as carrots or beets, cut off the root and stem ends. These can also harbor bacteria and should always be removed.

Depending on the type of pickles you are making, the produce can be left whole or cut into wedges, spears, slices, or even chunks. The key is to make all of the pieces the same shape, size, and thickness.

When a relish recipe calls for ground vegetables, you can use a meat grinder or a stand mixer with the grinder attachment to prepare the produce. Instead of grinding, you can also use a food processor to very finely chop the vegetables.

## Vinegar

White vinegar and cider vinegar are the traditional choices for canning pickles and relishes, but you can also use wine, herb, and fruit vinegars. The important factor for safe canning is that the vinegar must have an acidity level of at least 5%. Homemade vinegars, or vinegars with a lower acidity level, may allow the growth of harmful bacteria in the jars after processing. Never reduce the ratio or amount of vinegar in a pickle or relish recipe, which can make the recipe unsafe for canning. If you prefer pickles or relishes that are less tart, increase the amount of sugar in the recipe.

## Salt

Salt is an important ingredient in making pickles, particularly cucumber and squash pickles. Not only does it add flavor, but it also helps to draw liquid out of the vegetables so the vegetables can absorb more syrup, which produces better-tasting pickles. It also makes the pickles heavier so they are less likely to float in the jars after processing. While pickles may be safely prepared with a reduced amount of salt, or even no salt, the quality of cucumber, squash, and some other pickles will definitely suffer.

I recommend using canning or pickling salt to make pickles. In some cases, kosher salt may be substituted for canning salt. With iodized or non-iodized table salt, the non-caking additives in table salts may make the brine or syrup cloudy, though the pickles will still be safe to eat. Reduced-sodium salts may be used in pickle recipes, but they will produce similar results to using table salt. The pickles will also have a different taste than normally expected.

## Ingredients for Sauces and Salsas

### ✻ TOMATOES ✻

Tomatoes have been a staple canning ingredient for generations and are one of the most popular ingredients in a number of canned products. Roma tomatoes or other plum tomatoes are an excellent choice for making sauces and other preserves because they are significantly less juicy and have a firmer flesh than salad or slicing tomatoes. Plum tomatoes will yield a sauce with a strong flavor and smooth, thick texture. If a recipe calls for Roma or plum tomatoes, substituting other types may result in a thinner sauce, requiring additional cooking time, or softer tomato pieces in salsas. Beefsteak tomatoes also work well for some salsas and other preserves; however, salad or slicing tomatoes and many heirloom tomatoes break down when canned.

When choosing tomatoes, look for those that are fully ripe, firm to the touch with a slight give when pressed, and have a deep red color. Underripe tomatoes will lack flavor, while overripe or soft tomatoes can fall apart when canned and also contain a lot of juice, resulting in thin sauces or salsas. Tomatoes with dark-colored flesh will produce preserves with an intense flavor and a lovely red color.

Tomatoes have a low acidity level. To raise the acidity level for safe water bath canning, you'll need to add lemon juice, lime juice, or vinegar to the recipe. Be sure to use the specific type of acid called for in the ingredients. Never reduce the amount of acid in a tomato recipe, as this may encourage bacteria growth.

### ✻ CHILE PEPPERS ✻

You can adjust the amount and type of chile peppers called for in a recipe to suit your personal taste. If you like a lot of heat, increase the amount of peppers. For milder sauces or salsas, reduce it. I strongly recommend wearing gloves when handling and chopping chile peppers because the oils in hot peppers can cause chemical burns. Never touch your face, eyes, or mouth when working with chile peppers.

### ✻ ACID ✻

Never reduce the amount of acid in a sauce or salsa recipe. The vinegar, lemon juice, or lime juice is required for safe canning. If the recipe indicates bottled lemon juice or lime juice, do not substitute freshly squeezed juice for the bottled juice. Bottled juice has a consistent acidity level, which is required to raise the acidity level of the product high enough to make it safe for water bath processing.

# Barb's Bread-and-Butter Pickles

CONTRIBUTOR: BARBARA SCHALLER, MINNESOTA

MAKES 7 TO 8 PINTS

**4 quarts thinly sliced medium pickling cucumbers (about 25 cucumbers)**

**3 cups sliced onions (about 4 medium onions)**

**2 green bell peppers (or 1 red and 1 green pepper), chopped**

**3 cloves garlic, sliced**

**⅓ cup canning or pickling salt**

**5 cups granulated sugar**

**3 cups cider vinegar**

**2 tablespoons mustard seeds**

**1½ teaspoons celery seeds**

**1½ teaspoons ground turmeric**

This recipe was adapted from one Barbara found in an old *Better Homes & Gardens* cookbook. These pickles have been awarded nine blue ribbons in the 15 times she's entered them in competition. In 2001, they received a prize from the M. A. Gedney Company for the Best Pickle at the Minnesota State Fair. These are her husband's favorite pickles.

1. In a large container, combine the cucumbers, onions, bell peppers, and garlic. Add the salt. Cover with cracked ice and mix thoroughly. Let stand for 3 hours. Drain well.

2. In an 8-quart stainless steel stockpot, combine the sugar, cider vinegar, mustard seeds, celery seeds, and turmeric. Cook over medium-high heat, stirring constantly, until the sugar is completely dissolved. Add the drained cucumber mixture and heat just until the mixture comes to a boil. Remove the pot from the heat.

3. Using a slotted spoon, pack the pickles into hot jars, leaving ½-inch headspace. Ladle the hot syrup into the jars, covering the pickles and maintaining the ½-inch headspace. Remove any air bubbles. Wipe the jar rims and threads with a clean, damp paper towel. Apply hot lids and screw bands.

4. Process pint jars in a water bath canner for 10 minutes (see p. 24 for instructions). Remove from the water bath canner and let cool for 12 to 24 hours. Check the seals and remove the screw bands. Store jars in a cool, dry, dark place for up to 1 year.

# Corn Relish

CONTRIBUTOR: ALAN GRAVENOR, MARYLAND

MAKES 5 PINT JARS

**9 cups fresh corn kernels (12 to 15 large ears corn), or canned or frozen**

**2 cups chopped onions (2 to 3 medium onions)**

**1 cup chopped green bell peppers**

**½ cup chopped red bell peppers**

**1 cup granulated sugar**

**2 tablespoons table salt**

**1½ tablespoons celery seeds**

**1½ tablespoons mustard seeds**

**3 cups cider vinegar**

This is an easy, tasty relish that improves during storage. It's a great way to use summer corn and other fresh garden vegetables and is a nice accompaniment to a variety of meals, especially meat and potatoes. Chop the onions and peppers the same size as the corn kernels to create a uniform texture.

1. In an 8-quart stainless steel stockpot, combine the corn, onions, bell peppers, sugar, salt, celery seeds, mustard seeds, and vinegar. Bring to a boil over high heat, stirring frequently.

2. Cover, reduce the heat to medium low, and simmer for 15 minutes, stirring occasionally to prevent scorching. Remove the pot from the heat.

3. Ladle the relish into hot jars, leaving ½-inch headspace. Remove any air bubbles. Wipe the jar rims and threads with a clean, damp paper towel. Apply hot lids and screw bands.

4. Process pint jars in a water bath canner for 15 minutes (see p. 24 for instructions). Remove from the water bath canner and let cool for 12 to 24 hours. Check the seals and remove the screw bands. Store jars in a cool, dry, dark place for up to 1 year.

# Sweet and Tangy Tomato Relish

CONTRIBUTOR: BRENDA BUSTILLOS, TEXAS

MAKES ABOUT FIVE 8-OUNCE JARS OR 2 PINT JARS

**4 medium plum tomatoes, quartered**

**2 medium green bell peppers, seeds and membranes removed, quartered**

**1 cup coarsely chopped sweet onions (about 1 large onion)**

**1 cup coarsely chopped green cabbage**

**4 teaspoons kosher salt**

**1 cup granulated sugar**

**1 cup white vinegar**

**½ cup water**

**1 teaspoon mustard seeds**

**1 teaspoon celery seeds**

**1 teaspoon ground turmeric**

**SERVING SUGGESTION**

Use this delightful relish to season flaked tuna fish and cold summer salads or use as a backyard barbecue condiment for brats and dogs.

Brenda cannot imagine a game-day bratwurst or cold summer salad without this perfectly pleasing relish. Chow-chow fans beware—this may become your next go-to relish recipe!

1. Put the tomatoes, bell peppers, onions, and cabbage in a food processor and process until finely chopped. Drain.

2. Transfer the chopped vegetables to a medium bowl and sprinkle with the salt. Refrigerate, covered, for 4 to 12 hours.

3. Rinse the vegetables with cold water and drain well in a colander lined with a single layer of cheesecloth or in a large fine-mesh sieve.

4. In a 6-quart stainless steel stockpot, combine the sugar, vinegar, water, mustard seeds, celery seeds, and turmeric. Add the drained vegetables to the syrup. Bring the mixture to a boil over medium-high heat, stirring frequently. Reduce the heat and simmer, uncovered, for 10 to 15 minutes, or until thickened to the consistency you prefer. Remove the pot from the heat.

5. Ladle the relish into hot jars, leaving ½-inch headspace. Remove any air bubbles. Wipe the jar rims and threads with a clean, damp paper towel. Apply hot lids and screw bands.

6. Process 8-ounce jars in a water bath canner for 10 minutes; pint jars for 15 minutes (see p. 24 for instructions). Remove from the water bath canner and let cool for 12 to 24 hours. Check the seals and remove the screw bands. Store jars in a cool, dry, dark place for up to 1 year.

# Tomato Basil Sauce

CONTRIBUTOR: NANCY CHARRON, WASHINGTON

MAKES ABOUT 4 PINT JARS

**12 cups peeled and chopped ripe Roma or other plum tomatoes (8 to 9 pounds tomatoes)**

**10 cloves garlic, minced (about 1 head garlic)**

**4 cups chopped fresh basil leaves**

**8 shallots, minced**

**4 tablespoons red-wine vinegar**

**6 teaspoons granulated sugar**

**4 teaspoons freshly squeezed lemon juice**

**2 teaspoons pickling salt**

**1 teaspoon freshly ground coarse black pepper**

**8 scallions (including green tops), thinly sliced**

**1 can (12 ounces) tomato paste**

With the richness of plum tomatoes and fresh basil, this sauce captures the flavors of summer in a jar to enjoy all year long!

1. In an 8-quart stainless steel stockpot, combine the tomatoes, garlic, basil, shallots, vinegar, sugar, lemon juice, salt, and pepper.
2. Bring the mixture to a boil over medium-high heat, stirring frequently. Reduce the heat and boil gently, stirring frequently, for 5 minutes. Stir in the scallions and tomato paste, then return the mixture to a full boil. Remove the pot from the heat.
3. Ladle the sauce into hot jars, leaving ½-inch headspace. Remove any air bubbles. Wipe the jar rims and threads with a clean, damp paper towel. Apply hot lids and screw bands.
4. Process pint jars in a water bath canner for 35 minutes; quart jars for 40 minutes (see p. 24 for instructions). Remove from the water bath canner and let cool for 12 to 24 hours. Check the seals and remove the screw bands. Store jars in a cool, dry, dark place for up to 1 year.

# Roasted Corn and Sweet Pepper Salsa

CONTRIBUTOR: VALERIE J. FONG, CALIFORNIA

MAKES FIVE OR SIX 8-OUNCE JARS

**6 cups peeled, cored, seeded, and roughly chopped Roma or other plum tomatoes (4 to 5 pounds tomatoes)**

**6 cloves garlic, roughly chopped**

**4 cups fresh white corn kernels (about 8 ears corn)**

**3 bell peppers (1 red, 1 orange, and 1 yellow), seeded and diced**

**1 red onion, chopped**

**2 shallots, finely chopped**

**3 tablespoons olive oil**

**1 cup red-wine vinegar**

**¼ cup balsamic vinegar**

**¼ cup freshly squeezed lemon juice**

**2 tablespoons granulated sugar**

**1 tablespoon table salt**

**1 teaspoon freshly ground black pepper**

**1 can (6 ounces) tomato paste**

**¼ cup finely chopped fresh flat-leaf parsley**

This blend of roasted fresh corn and sweet peppers creates a savory salsa that is a delightful addition to a summer outdoor meal. By roasting the vegetables first, their natural sugars really come through and complement the rich flavor of the balsamic vinegar.

While the salsa is terrific with chips and guacamole, it is also excellent on a hamburger in place of regular relish.

1. In a blender, purée the tomatoes and garlic. Set aside.

2. In a large skillet over medium-high heat, sauté the corn, bell peppers, onions, and shallots in olive oil until the vegetables are slightly roasted and lightly charred, 3 to 5 minutes.

3. In an 8-quart stainless steel stockpot, combine the tomato purée and roasted corn mixture. Stir until well blended, then add the red-wine vinegar, balsamic vinegar, lemon juice, sugar, salt, black pepper, and tomato paste. Stir until blended.

4. Bring the mixture to a simmer over medium heat and cook for about 10 minutes, stirring occasionally. Add the parsley and cook for another 2 minutes. Remove the pot from the heat.

5. Ladle the salsa into hot jars, leaving ½-inch headspace. Remove any air bubbles. Wipe the jar rims and threads with a clean, damp paper towel. Apply hot lids and screw bands.

6. Process 8-ounce jars in a water bath canner for 10 minutes (see p. 24 for instructions). Remove from the water bath canner and let cool for 12 to 24 hours. Check the seals and remove the screw bands. Store jars in a cool, dry, dark place for up to 1 year.

# * Fruits & Vegetables *

Canning fruits and vegetables is a wonderful way to preserve an abundant orchard or garden harvest so you can enjoy a taste of summer sunshine all year long. An assortment of canned fruits and vegetables on the pantry shelf helps make meal preparation faster and easier, too.

# Canning Fruit

You can enjoy home-canned fruit on its own; as an alternative to syrup on pancakes, waffles, and French toast; as a topping for ice cream; or in baking recipes. For the best color, flavor, and texture, use beautiful, unblemished fruit at the peak of ripeness.

### ❋ PREPARING FRUIT ❋

Rinse the fruit under cool running water and drain well on paper towels. To prevent fruit deterioration, only rinse and prepare enough for one canning batch at a time. Most fruit should be peeled before canning, including peaches, pears, apples, and pineapple. Apricots are usually canned with the peels on because it helps the fruit maintain its shape during processing. Delicate fruits that should not be peeled include cherries, grapes, and berries.

Depending on the type of fruit you are canning, it can be packed whole, halved, sliced, or cut into spears or chunks. For the best result, select fruit that is about the same size and cut into pieces that are uniform in shape and appearance. To prevent light-colored fruits from turning brown after peeling, soak the fruit in an antioxidant solution before canning. You can find antioxidant crystals, or fruit preservatives, in grocery stores alongside the canning supplies. Follow the manufacturer's instructions for use and length of soaking time.

### ❋ PACKING JARS ❋

The most common way to pack fruit into the jars is using the hot pack method—boil a mix of sugar and water to create a syrup, then add the fruit and cook briefly before packing it into the jars. This allows the fruit to absorb some of the sugar and also to become more pliable so it can be packed snugly into the jars. A tighter pack means the fruit is less likely to float in the jars after canning. After being packed into the jars, the fruit is covered with the hot syrup. Fruit may also be packed into the jars raw and covered with a boiling syrup. This is known as a raw pack and is the best method for canning delicate fruits, such as grapes, cherries, and berries.

Fruit can be canned in sugar syrup, fruit juice, or even water. I prefer to use a light to medium sugar syrup for canning fruit. The sugar will help the fruit maintain its shape and texture, and also preserve and enhance the flavor. Fruit packed in heavy syrup is more likely to float in the jar because the higher sugar concentration makes the syrup heavier than the fruit.

# Canning Vegetables

For the best results, can vegetables as soon as possible after picking or purchase from your local farmers' market. Fresh, crisp, young, tender vegetables yield the best canned products. Large or fully matured vegetables contain more water, have larger seeds, and are more likely to turn soft and break down when canned. Depending on the type or variety, overripe vegetables can either be mushy or starting to dry out. Bruised or damaged vegetables may contain bacteria or excessive enzymes, which can lead to spoilage.

### ✻ PACKING JARS ✻

As with fruit, there are two methods used to pack vegetables into jars for canning—the hot pack method and the raw pack method.

In the hot pack method, the vegetables are cooked in simmering water for a few minutes to partially cook and also to allow air trapped inside the vegetable pieces to escape and be replaced with liquid. Without the air, the vegetables are more pliable and heavier, permitting more vegetables to be packed into the jars and reducing the chances of them floating in the jars after processing. The raw pack method is just what it sounds like. Raw vegetables are packed snugly into the jars and then covered with boiling water.

For both packing methods, salt may be added to each jar of vegetables for seasoning, but it is not required for safe food preservation. You can add up to ½ teaspoon salt per pint jar or 1 teaspoon salt per quart jar. Canning or pickling salt is recommended to prevent the liquid in the jar from turning cloudy.

No matter which packing method you use, the headspace for all vegetable packs is 1 inch. This allows room for the vegetables to expand and the liquid to boil during pressure canner processing. If there is too little headspace in the jar, some of the liquid will be forced out of the jar as the contents heat. If there is too much headspace, not enough air will be vented from the jar and the jar and lid may not form a tight vacuum seal.

### ✻ PROCESSING VEGETABLES ✻

Vegetables are low-acid foods and must be processed in a pressure canner. During pressure canning, the internal temperature of the jars will reach 240°F, which can only be reached in a pressure canner. (Jars processed in a water bath canner will only reach an internal temperature of 212°F, which is too low to safely process low-acid foods.) Except for tomatoes canned with bottled lemon juice or vinegar, pressure canning is the only safe method for canning vegetables and vegetable products.

# Peach Halves

CONTRIBUTOR: MELINDA REESE, VIRGINIA

MAKES ABOUT SIX 1-QUART JARS

**2 quarts water**

**2 cups granulated sugar**

**10 to 12 pounds round unblemished peaches**

**NOTE:**

Jars or bottles with wire-bail-attached glass lids and rubber seals are not endorsed for canning use by the USDA. Contents should be refrigerated and used within a few days.

Perfect peaches are a challenge to can because if you pack them too tight, they'll break, and if you don't pack them tight enough, they'll float.

1. In a 4-quart stainless steel stockpot, combine the water and sugar. Bring the mixture to a boil over medium-high heat, stirring constantly until the sugar is completely dissolved. Boil the syrup for 1 minute, then reduce the heat to low and keep hot until needed.

2. Fill an 8-quart stainless steel stockpot with water and bring to a boil. Cut a small X on the bottom of the peaches, then dip them into the boiling water for 30 seconds to 1 minute to loosen the skins. Transfer to a bowl of ice water for 2 minutes to cool and stop the cooking. Drain well.

3. Cut the peaches into even halves. Remove the pits and peels, then rinse and drain well.

4. Pack the peaches, cavity side down, into hot jars, leaving 1/2-inch headspace. Overlap the peaches from side to side to create a pretty appearance and snug pack.

5. Ladle the hot syrup into the jars, covering the peaches and maintaining the 1/2-inch headspace. Remove any air bubbles. If necessary, add more syrup to maintain to headspace. Wipe the jar rims and threads with a clean, damp paper towel. Apply hot lids and screw bands.

6. Process pint jars in a water bath canner for 25 minutes; quart jars for 30 minutes (see p. 24 for instructions). Remove from the water bath canner and let cool for 12 to 24 hours. Check the seals and remove the screw bands. Store jars in a cool, dry, dark place for up to 1 year.

# Vegetable Soup

CONTRIBUTOR: JANET GAMBLE, IDAHO

**MAKES 12 TO 13 QUARTS**

**4 quarts peeled and quartered tomatoes (7 to 9 pounds)**

**4 quarts peeled and chopped potatoes (8 to 10 pounds)**

**6 cups peeled and chopped carrots (10 to 14 carrots)**

**4 cups cut or snapped green beans (1-inch pieces) (1½ to 2 pounds)**

**4 onions, chopped**

**2 cups chopped celery (4 to 6 stalks)**

**18 cups water**

**12 beef soup base cubes**

**1 cup pearl barley**

**2 tablespoons table salt**

**1 tablespoon Italian seasoning**

**1 teaspoon Mrs. Dash® seasoning (optional)**

**½ teaspoon freshly ground black pepper**

**NOTE:**

Soup is shown on p. 44. Jars or bottles with wire-bail-attached glass lids and rubber seals are not endorsed for canning use by the USDA. Contents should be stored in the refrigerator and used within a few days.

Homemade vegetable soup is so much better than soup out of a can from the grocery store. This one is delicious! For vegetable beef, Janet adds some cooked ground beef to the soup when she heats it up.

1. In a 16- to 20-quart stainless steel stockpot, combine all of the ingredients in the order listed and stir to combine. Bring the mixture to a boil over medium-high heat, stirring frequently. Reduce the heat, cover, and simmer for 30 minutes, stirring occasionally. The vegetables should be just tender but not soft. Remove the pot from the heat.

2. Ladle the soup into hot pint jars, leaving 1-inch headspace. Remove any air bubbles. Wipe the jar rims and threads with a clean, damp paper towel. Apply hot lids and screw bands.

3. Process pint jars for 60 minutes and quart jars for 75 minutes at 11 pounds of pressure in a dial-gauge pressure canner or at 10 pounds of pressure in a weighted-gauge pressure canner (see p. 26 for instructions).

4. After the processing time is complete, remove the canner from the heat. Let the pressure return to zero before removing the jars from the canner. Let cool for 12 to 24 hours. Check the seals and remove the screw bands. Store jars in a cool, dry, dark place for up to 1 year.

**TIP**

If you don't have a stockpot big enough to hold the whole batch, you can use two stockpots or divide the ingredients in half and make a smaller batch.